CHOSEN

CHOSEN

Poems by Toni Thomas

BRICK ROAD

POETRY PRESS

Front cover photo credit: © James Luciana

Library of Congress Control Number: 2011937810
ISBN-13: 978-0-9835304-1-1

Published by Brick Road Poetry Press
P. O. Box 751
Columbus, GA 31902-0751
www.brickroadpoetrypress.com

Brick Road logo by Dwight New

To my children, Ahven and Fergus,
for their endless love, patience, and support,
my parents who gifted me with life and gave me
opportunities they were never able to have themselves,
Janet Healy for her enduring friendship and love as a sister,
and with thanks to Ilya Kaminsky, Galway Kinnell,
Sharon Olds, John Haislip, Robert Hass and many others
for their care and encouragement along the way

Acknowledgments

Grateful acknowledgement is made to the editors of the following publications in which some of these poems first appeared (in slightly different versions):

The Chariton Review: "For Those of Us Who Persist to Contemplate Magic in a Damped Down World"

Cold Mountain Review: "History Lesson"

Gingko Tree Review: "Lucky in Love"

HazMat Review: "We Corner Hope"

Penwood Review: "Marius Shamey, My Catechism Teacher"

Poetry East: "Chosen"

Potomac Review: "Pink—Such a Frittery Color"

Prairie Schooner: "Blue Danube"

Purple Patch (England): "The Grey Eye of Success"

Slipstream: "Mary Jo"

Studio (Australia): "I Wanted God" and "My Brother Tells Me"

White Pelican Review: "My Birthday"

CONTENTS

Part One *Secret Fragilities*

Part Two *A Flaming Angel in Steel Shoes*

Part Three *Little Dagger of Nothing*

Part Four *The Perilous Undertakings
of the Everyday World*

Part Five *The Body's Lasting Allegiance to Snow*

Poet is a voice, I say, like Icarus
whispering to himself as he falls.

Yes, my life as a broken branch in the wind
hits the Northern ground.
I am writing now a history of snow,
the lamplight bathing the ships
that sail across the page.

But on certain afternoons
the Republic of Psalms opens up
and I grow frightened that I haven't lived, died, not
enough
to scratch this ecstasy into vowels, hear
splashes of clear, biblical speech.

from *Dancing in Odessa*

—Ilya Kaminsky

Part One

Secret Fragilities

.

While the Car Crash Was Still Receding from Her Mind's Imaginary Aquarium

Majestic—maybe that's what she wanted
dangerous even
as if bad had its aspirin-coated appeal
dark licorice stories to tell
like the one-eyed psychic
wedged in black
who lived up past the sound
had a cue of customers waiting out
games of solitaire by the door.

It was her second life
after the car crash.
The plastic surgeon's apocalyptic
calling to reconstruct and stitch back her face.
The months of white bandages, work leave
marriage separation, the one-room studio apartment
she succored with her prayer book
the exact morsels of dinner by the bed.
Nobody could accuse her of being fat anymore
or materialistic or pedestrian as neat married
women in pantyhose clutching stiff umbrellas
to ward off the rain.
Her ecclesiastical life burning.
Sweet on the bread sticks.
How many cups of tea, cigarettes
to collapse a day
wring it out white eyelet
on the sloped clothesline.

Everything kept raining
down on her—
God and light
unimaginable suitors
stilted houses
under which the sea keeps heaving.

We Made Love in the Japanese Garden

the two of us loitering
in the corner
away from the tourists.
Lulled amid the bamboo screens
pools of carp, gabled roof lines.
Two geese flying.
The drip drip drip of slow water
from the bamboo pipe
rupturing the pond's smooth skin.

You said you'd love me forever
but did not want this child.
She of the secret bessoming.
I made a pact with God
that what was lost would someday
come back as hyacinth.

Eight years later it takes hours
to land in Beijing
make the journey south to you.
You are beautiful, my daughter
four-years-old, love tangerines
are ringworm infested, have a bald spot
an island where lustrous
black tresses long to be.
I have painted you stories for your
journey to me.
The dark sea, the surreptitious boat
me trying to reach you.
My sad hands empty as pigeons.
The hummingbird's cool breath.

You speak Cantonese.
At first the body's own language of love
must make a nest for us.
Later, my small painting pegged to your wall
you ask why it took so long
to reach you.
I talk about big squalls, shipwrecks
nights with no stars in them
the boat with its capsizable keel
how I bargained with God
to keep a watchful eye on you—
oldest girl
three and a half long years in the orphanage
told God that I would treasure you always
like the orange carp in the happy pond

told God I would make good
on my treasonous past
the man who won his sensible way
over my vestibules
the secret transgression
the knowledge of fishes.
That what is lost
I shall will back to us
as psalm.

The Grey Eye of Success Casts a Halo
over the Coast's Otherwise Sodden Geometry

The nights here are calm as
cursed cotton
calculated school rooms.
Everyone asleep in the satin sheets
of their beds.
Transients marooned in another
coast town
where the coffee is cheap
and the streets are lined with a string
of rundown bungalows
almost nobody owns.

I will be here a week.
As if placid is calling me.
People who saunter with their french pastries
reliable second homes.

One morning will I wake up
stunned by the sea's benevolence
the trees' refusal to grow old here?
Does the moon ever miss a beat
desert her well-off husband
and run?

Reluctance Caves in My Head's Fortitude and I Listen to the Rain Weeping

The air is dense here. Spring loaded.
February marching into April
with its tight fist.
I pitchfork time
watch it squirm
my opinions desolate
as shotgunned birds
the past that never quite comes
clean in our hands.

You can shine polished teeth in this neighborhood
shop for hours and never get tired of it
the hands of the Hispanic workers
pruning your bloodthirsty roses
tying up half-bent peonies
hauling Hoovers over
the house's inside terrain.

Some avenues go in circles
never get anywhere.
The head forgets to caress
the seizure of roses.
My feet want to lead me
into another landscape
stunned with rosemary
the purple crowns of the chive
humming their way past easy happiness
with a rain-soaked tongue.

The past will never come back.
My appetites may nail me
to the wall again and again.
I reach past insolvency
pin on that other lullaby
that burns in the trees.

Lucky in Love

that's the card the fortune teller
turned up for her.
Not a dime a dozen.
She left smelling of jasmine
bought two brownies on the way home
waited for the miraculous
to enter her door
clear the rubble from her life
stay there.

It took two months
before he arrived.
Ate her carrots and Brussels sprouts
romantic notions
didn't complain about them
as if even a stunted eye has a right
to heaven.

One year later he proposed to her.
The burning bush of it.
The crown of thorns he presented
for her hair
as if marriage was a two-headed penny
luck on one side where love
lights a fire over some sturdy bed
bad news on the other
fallow fields
sorghum dried up in your hands
the rough and the smooth of it
the sumptuous waylaid with the lead.

You will crown your life with a
lasting achievement,
that's the card that turned up for her.
Three years later.
The fortune teller's weak lamp
the parlor's rose-flecked monotony.
He would not be the lasting achievement.
She knew that.
He was not what he had been.
Love wore its torn envelope
and soiled seersucker.

The sheets all sensibly laundered.
Her blankety blankety blank
stirring.
As if *forgive us our sins*
is just a church platitude
for fallen angels
and what is sin, after all
and what is matrimony
and what is this pallor
slowly overtaking her body's
monkish allegiances?

A Friend of Mine Walks Her Poodle
through a Shop Window
Admits Impermanence

Glass shards scattered everywhere.
The red snap purse smothered in a Braille
of diamonds.
The window fallen in on you.
The sheer weight of it.
As if we had stumbled from our steel throat
and dogs were a nemesis to heaven.

That day—the fiction lifted.
The plaster and bandages
the sutures and sirens.
Afterwards the poodle's coat
grown back long, curly
in need of a pedigree.

You who never disavowed your master
accepted her as undeniably the woman
with the leash wired to her wrist
accepts now that life can scald us
that every fixed filament
has its secret fragilities to bear.

I Was Told Dick Traber

was a tired show
that he used to make people laugh
so hard they wet their pants
stumbled into alleys with
no shoes on
but that was years ago
when the old vaudeville acts
came to town
and now he is the star of nobody's show
crushing ice in the kitchen on the fifth floor
of the retirement center where folks
with few resources, no family
get sent to stay.

My daughter's doing a school project.
She is eight. Comes from China.
Spent the first four years in an orphanage
looking after a toddler, mingling with
the toothless old people on the second floor.
She has delicate bouquets in her heart.
A love for animals. Quiet ways that don't
need to broadcast themselves.

It was back in February her class started this.
Going once a week for a couple of hours to
the retirement center up in Oregon City.
A dreary building, small windows looking out
on a high traffic road.
Sometimes she brings our collie, Poco,
drags him up to Dick Traber's room

on the fifth floor.
I wait in the lobby.
Watch the coffee trays come and go.

My daughter notices Mr. Traber is old.
Smells of tobacco. That his hands shake
when he shows her his photographs
in the worn frames.
In April she gathers sprigs of lavender
wraps them in foil
brings them on the Thursday visit
to brighten the table.
Takes pictures of our cat, the new puppy
says Mr. Traber pins them on the
back side of his door.

She comes home with comedy routines
a few soft shoe shuffles
worries herself we have too much
and some people have too little.
She does this for three months—twelve weeks
of visits—Dick Traber gets used to it.

One day the tiny knock on the door
doesn't come.
The children have already mailed their
thank you notes and well wishes
for a nice spring.
My daughter's soccer practice begins.
The neighbor girl three up no longer
goes to childcare
comes over with dolls in her hands.
Mr. Traber knows

not to expect much.
That the world is a carousel
of soft shoe shuffling.

At 2pm Mabel comes in with the usual
afternoon meds.
Stops back at 6pm before going off day shift.
Dick Traber takes out his cards.
The pack with the vanishing aces.
Shuffles them in his one good hand.

Blue Danube

You buy happiness
with a steel wick
crowbar it to an unyielding clothesline
as if the curse of desolation means
a loss of buffed shoes
a hint of want
that drives wormholes into the
carefully etched wood.

September comes with its thrifty tongue
the fragile egg-cup
the fusion of school days, boxed lunches
dinner with the pot boiling
lust left to drag its guttural grey
between the length of the
sandwich bread.
Our love grows apostolic
cramped on a thin lip.
My hemlines' perfect luminaries are bleeding.

A desert of blue envelopes
elopes with the wind.
The children grow docile in their tidy shoes.
Something keeps running away with my feet.
You witness my half-sung body
my refusal to be slain by safe hands
and I sing
All the world's a crock of shattered Blue Danube.
My mother sang that to me.
In my deepest heart I am fleeing
what can't be born here.

Nine Years after the Abortion

I call you *the sphinx with the shrunken shoes*.
Nobility gone awry in a blighted world
a once river of mysterium
til you heeded all things that insisted
to be answered
and answered them.
Such proclivity.
Such stillness.

I was pregnant again.
In the middle of a custody suit
over our three-year-old boy child.
It was easier to abolish her from the table.
Put it down to bad timing
my lack of money
the efficient way your mind works.

Consummation of what?
Now you get only the spare change
I can willingly leave by the back door.
The world is a square tub
with heavy porcelain in it
refuses to give back what it takes
refuses to let the trillium run wild
over the flask of trees
the invisible foraging.

You tap your hand over plenty
and let it sing there.
That other gold nightingale

in the tree.
Her black patent shoes shining blind
over every transparent thing.

After You Dismiss *Jane Eyre* with the Caveat of Your Cold Hand

This marriage has stung me
where it hurts most
formidable ecclesiastics
the center of the bed
where passion turns its brown face
away from the moon
dismisses hope
the yellow chiffon dress
she sang in.

When I question
your suitability as a lover
the sun answers
bleached umbrella stands
peeled paint
the havoc a July heat wave
can tender
every room fan sold out in the stores
my body mercurial
melted to metal rungs of the fire escape
trying to find a stairway to paradise
imagining happiness
is just a hair's breadth away
a redeemed apple
an abbreviation that turns
whole as the zero
I bathe in my hand.

If I Were Clever Enough

I could reinvent heaven
the corsaged lapel
the broken in toe-shoes
the day never needing to right itself
on benign knees
and axed thistle.

I knock light out of the side table.
Ask the geranium to limp its way
back to life, proposition my husband
to notice my champagne legs
the bruises that keep accumulating
like cut glass on a strident sofa.

My son says happiness
is a foot long sub sandwich
with chicken and lots of bacon.
He is eleven.
Measures the world in mouthfuls.
Draws cartoons to satirize what he can't
understand.
I measure hope like a hand grenade
that can explode in our faces
decide that bravery
is a measure of letting defeat
find a place to live in us
dilapidated shoes lulled to sleep
under park benches
bird-pooped awnings where

cups of cappuccino
stay sacrosanct in the rain.

Buckled clothesline
are you bent under the weight
of so many stories to tell?

Small Voice

June sits like a sunken equator
with its careful benevolence.
A few button-top raspberries
on the bushes.
The spinach plants bolting
their green leaves remnant
of what might have survived here
the basil decimated
the six tomato plants, pumpkin and squash vines
sensible in the measured girth of their growth.

A girl could forget her past.
Never try to ransack heaven.
Make the day just the day just the day.
Never scribe corridors of blue ink
up her arm
the stenciled deliberations.
As if no flies buzz through this door
and no one has ever lapsed deliverance
from the body's illicit exuberance.
The rows and rows of cos lettuce
will gather their tight heads
like the nuns whose black habits
covered their arms' tyrannies.

There will be no indecency
just June bugs

the skunk cabbage's histrionic yellow thrones
the manageable day
so manageable
all the Western world hard at work
a triumph of decay
a buttonhole of shine.

An Arc of Chintz Floats

over the floor's loose shoes.
I dream of islands.
Sun damaged men.
A rigging of sails
my indiscriminate life swelling.
As if a rumba can unpeel
vagrant hips, plant ice cubes
in the cleavage
the world has made of me.

It is Sunday.
Holiness invades the courtyard
plumes the bougainvillea
til they will stand up to anything.
You whisper nothing in my ear.
The prerogative of privilege to
annex what God sends.

Dance with me.
The hem of my dress keeps lengthening.

We Corner Hope

let it hang from a noose
by the side table.
My wedding ring climbs
my left finger
crushes the prosperity of roses.

It is December
a loop of red globes
the obscene raking of toys
from the store shelves.
Christ in the belly of Mary.
Forlorn stars staked up on the
manger's abbreviated walls.
The shepherds' simple redress
no systematic articulation
of the scheme of things.

The man I married sidesteps nuance
the riot of lace
stickpins fancy to his kitchen epitaphs
the ceremony of the Polish cookies
as if the fiction of powdered sugar
the yardstick of baking
can swab hope to our faces.

It is the Northwest.
The rain keeps pawing.
Cookie canisters pile up on anonymous thrones.
The day is squeezed into the weight of big meals.
The children beg me for card games

craft projects, someone to visit, roller skating
a Santa Claus poem.
Everything I long for slips silently away.
The man in my bed stockpiles headlines
cookie batter, the betrayal of roses.
How many wheelbarrows does it take
to carry a house load of winter
to avalanche my body
in the pure white deuteronomy
of snow?

A Love Poem

Someday will I come back reborn
churned as butter
thick and creamy
paying homage to the wood planks
of the barrel, the children
who have spun me
with the diligence of their hands
turned ordinary milk
into a homage
for the toast's lathing.

December can be gruesome
materialistic as sin
mows down field grass
sends a secret plague between
the branches of tree ornaments.
Heavy as the boot soles of those
who need to conquer everything
expend the ribbon and lace
til we define ourselves
as plagues and pendants
the virtue of efficient hands.

Let us be derelict then.
You and I. Lovers.
Unconquerable. Grass-stained.
The naked exuberance of our feet's indentures
squishing mud, raising up
the history of lost bottle caps

pine cones, pebbles, maiden fern
the ancient skunk cabbage
nobody owns.
Maybe we won't be so foreign then.
A massacre of days with this other
purse towing.
All the birds who sanctify our life
from an invisible throne.

Part Two

A Flaming Angel in Steel Shoes

When She Slurred Her Words

like a drunken sailor
they never understood she had a head injury
from the stray car that threw her body
off the roadway 25 years ago
put her in a coma
made her have to learn how to walk again
the length of her proclamations
grown monotone
flat as pancakes in a disinterested world.
That's why only Christ could save her
and we place all our stock in him.

My mother and I move every few years
but she's always wanted me
to rise up on pointe, see tiptoe
over every fence line.
Since age three she's been finding ways
for me to take the ballet
seeks out doctors to figure out why
my muscular body
won't conform to a thin wick.
Begs relatives, takes out loans
on her disability checks
sends me away summers—
Wisconsin, California, Idaho, Oregon,
stakes her life on the power of my legs.

No one can find me here
lost in the lines of perfect dancers
their whittled teenage bodies and thin breath.

Lost in the pallor of rows and rows of pointe shoes.
My pink satin bands singed to keep the ends from fraying
crisscrossed carefully about my legs.
They say that necessity makes a mockery
of dissolution
that anyone can stand up resolute
in a tail wind with enough grace.
I dance on air
make excuses
translate my mother's strange tongue.
We are exiled from one dance studio
after another.
Move on. Move west.
Our new apartment grows moss
barely keeps above flood line.

I hold the world on my shoulders
know the dark is the dark is the dark
know that light saves us
that God is watching me
reliable as the laces of shoes
clear as the voice I will
give back to him
in my mother's true tongue.

Nobody Recovered Much

when Joyce R. stepped onto
the Stark Street Bridge, hoisted
her legs over the steel girders
and vanished away.
My mother wrote a card of condolence
talked about our fond recollections
my memory of the rhinestone barrettes
Joyce anchored in her hair.

The truth is—I never knew her.
Not really.
She sat on the yearbook committee
was literary editor for three years.
Wore black tights with snug-fitting
waistbands.
If she had a boyfriend none of us
ever saw him.
Joyce R. got more than her fair share
of laughs when she showed up alone
senior prom night wearing a pleated skirt
and scuffed grey shoes.
Neil W. condemned her as *something frazzled
the wind dragged in.*
I don't remember anybody
coming up to congratulate her
when she won the speech contest
spieled on and on about *the Holocaust, 911,
the Patriot's Act
citizen's rights being trampled
if we're not careful these days.*

Her father died when she was seven.
Something about the wrong meds.
We all knew that
knew it was just Joyce and her mother
in the bungalow on Seventh.
Mrs. R. has worked for thirteen years in
the school cafeteria at Carson Elementary.
Probably brings home decent pay.

There's no excuse for taking your life.
I told my mother that the other day.
Doesn't matter how weird you may feel
how many times you don't get picked
there's always hope out there
God wielding his fiery chariot
picking up every lost thing.

Our minister, Doctor Bob, says
the saved are always the obedient
and swift in the eyes of the Lord
that in the end the chosen
never go perishing in the rain
can't help but ride hotrod
over every rank thing.

Jesus Saved George Williams

three doors down from us.
He quit the bottle. Started sending
repentance notes to Ruth and the kids.
Swept out the garage, had a yard sale
replaced kitchen formica.
There was a lot of church-going after that.
Wednesday prayer group.
Men's revival suppers. Pentecostal meetings.
My dad grew impatient
said George's handball game went to pieces
with all the formica being laid.
Ruth moved back in over spring break with the kids.
Dug a trench and planted two even rows of begonias.
Shoved the metal legs of white geese
into the dirt by the bird feeder.

When the day of the annual Fourth of July
        block party arrived
George insisted we use his front yard.
There were burgers, dill pickles, my dad's
        German potato salad
hot dogs from Celeste's butcher shop
and enough potato chips to fill a sandbox.
My mother started playing
those old Ella Fitzgerald tunes.
She was in her white pedal pushers and midriff top
her bare feet tapping their own secret rhythms
        into the grass.
I remember Ruth in and out busying herself
with hot dog buns, spatulas, George's request

for another beer. I remember George half-crazed
with Fourth of July happiness.
The way he bossed his kids
wouldn't take any guff from them
how they had to eat every morsel that landed
    on their plates,
the way he scolded Ruth
when she finally grabbed her first lemonade
sank down into one of the chairs.

Mostly I remember George. How he turned out
to be quite the dancer.
A can of ale pressed in one hand.
Come evening coaxing my mama again and again
up and out of her seat.
My father in the elsewheres.

George telling everybody to *pipe down* when
a song he fancied came on.
His empty hand roaming over my mama's spine
her waist
my mama trying to be gracious
redirect his arms
as if redemption
snatches up the carefree bird at the feeder
places it safely in a glass cage
for its own good
reannoints the surety
of our Jesus-proclaimed hands.

Marius Shamey, My Catechism Teacher

once said when you contemplate the ocean
hold a pebble in your hand
so you know how small a being can be
and how great the waters around you.
I was ten.
Lived inland.
Away from boats
salmon-gutted decks
crab fishermen whose hands guided the cages
sullied themselves in dark water.
Already felt invisible
the pebble nobody sees
on the anonymous sand.

We ate fish on Fridays.
Cod wrapped in brown paper at the
Grand Union on Hillside Avenue.
Unwrapped by the white hands of my mother
who drank so much salt water
when she was four
her eyes grew liquid blue as wild herons.
All summer when she was 18
her bronzed lifeguard body
combed Horsetail Beach.
She learned to rescue perishable things
swim out farther than the rest.

I don't swim.
Am afraid of rip tides, pools of jellyfish
swarms of seaweed
over-tanned, industrious hands
efficient women with webbed feet
who sidestep the rain.
Know that malevolence has many forms.
Sometimes my glass eye
pretends the world is made of softer stuff
that I am floating in an ocean
so benevolent no one vanishes away.
My arms a tinsel of big sail
keen in a sharp wind
ruffled in still time
unhitched to any mean thing.

My body clenchable
permeable
as the smallest stone
God heaves up for me.

My Father is Born Again Three Times

before he dies.
Swears that the church saved him
that Christ came down
wrapped him in flaming wings,
erased the desire for beer
from his lips
set him right in the world.

Afterwards, my father offers up prayer books,
hot dog barbeques, Scout jamborees
where my mother's lace-lustered
hands used to be.
My mama in her slinky black dresses and
split-leather shoes.
My father leading us down the aisle to be
swallowed by God's love—
his arm raising *hallelujahs*
his fists that ward off evil
crush beetles
split in two my belligerent brother's baseball bat
vanquish every mean thing
til we are waspless nests in the wind.

My mother stops stringing
colored lights across the lawn
baiting dad with her penchant for strawberries
tells me to listen to my father,
that Jesus will save me.
Over the years my mother
eats more fudge marble ice cream

bowls of it
avoids damnation
my father's strident hand
til we are trimmed
as sweet grass
harmonizing
with our litter of kittens
our youth group
neat buckled shoes.

Our shiny tongues that
step over every vile thing
never go perishing
in the rain.

Chosen

In Fargo, North Dakota no one
measured the length of my life
by the line of the world's grievances.
I spelt Christ into the corners of my day.
Drifted in snow fields, slid on ice
slept in my mother's cramped apartment
amidst the resurrection song all sinners
come to with a chastened tongue.

Fifteen years pass by on clutched knees.
I am chosen. Forgiven. Ordained. Blessed.
Hallelujah comes out of every church pew.
I close my eye around derision
eat up the sun
keep my head above water
above water
til the world waits for me
a flaming angel in steel shoes
my mother molten on disability checks.
There is nothing I can't do
with the perspicuity
the iron resolve
of God's wings.

Prophecy

If there is a curse
it is the curse of prophecy
of seeing the yellow-stained eye
overtake the world's sweetmeat
seeing the drowned boy
the wreck of a marriage
that busts out doors
sirens police—
and for this she paid dearly
every night
restless of sleep
by day wallpapering hope over
the torn-down places
watching the lives of others
fall apart
get put back together
in imaginary fistfuls.

She starts sending notes.
Handwritten at first.
Keep your boy away from water,
or *your marriage needs a stout measure*
of oriental poppies, Sunday matinees
with love in them,
don't go to work on the 13th—stay
home all day.
She takes to typing the messages
delivers them anonymously
by nightfall
doesn't notice that no one pays

much attention to them.
Wants to believe others
will heed an earnest homily,
that faithful intentions wear the wind
in their hair, decline deceitfulness
that God raises his treacherous hand
over every deft thing
brings a season of green floods
to cataract the rain.

Part Three

Little Dagger of Nothing

How Blue Is the Worship of Your Tongue's Christenings

The retreat center hums with adolescent
t-shirts saying *He is the ONE*.
Come evening clusters of boys with red faces
girls in snug midriff tops drift their way
past our house down to the river
toss stones through the water's thin skin.

It is Sunday.
The catechisms and incantations
of the chosen
cloy the air.
Their voices run sure-footed
through our bed of iris
the nasturtium we will lade
onto soup and lick with our thirsty tongues.

Have I been placed here to rant and rave
be converted into the proposition of eternal light
own up to my own sinfulness
read the slogans tacked weekly on the church's
billboards—
Only God holds the key to happiness.
Trust not your own devices
lest the world leads you into damnation.
Deny sin, be as a little lamb and come onto me.

I pin wet shorts up on our clothesline.
Skim the bugs off the rubber pool
my children will paddle in with their purple fins.
Nothing seems evil to them

telescopic
groping as starved hamsters left to rot
in sinewy cages.

My children devise miracles out of
the wormwood
fairy kingdoms snugged into rock ledges.
Inflate the black inner tube, the yellow giraffe.
I finish skimming off bugs, pine needles with the net.
Unplug the filter.
See how the chlorine tablet erases haze
turns the water clear,
remember how blurry
muddy the world can be
how much sorrow lays forgotten
behind mall parking lots
how my children love this green paradise
the blue blue water
they splash and fall in
gulp, spit out
with their unloathesome tongues.

If there is sin
it is a feckless creation
not yet born in their world
maybe only later will they learn that
green sea monsters don't always float and foam
and rise gently onto the water's slick tongue
that there are holes so big
people sink in them
and sometimes nothing
not even God

gets retrieved
for love or money
with the weight of our hands.

I Think of Eloise

who wore her matchless
navy coat into the harshest downpours.
Trundled in yellow boots
was never able to forget the past
her father's stub-toed homilies
the sealed envelope of her mother's words
never able to leave her own fence
join us on our way up the road
to the Immaculate Conception School
where Sister Rosalind would daily check our hands
search for nail dirt, mouth scum
inform us of the formidable cost of sin
the weight of it
how *every good thing gets plucked*
from our heart's deliverance
when a being
spits in the eye of God
and walks away.

Eloise was my neighbor four houses down.
She never fell from God's grace
never made it to her sixteenth birthday
died when the car she was traveling in
swerved off the road.
As if God needed her before the rest.

I don't remember Eloise ever dancing
around maypoles

swimming in clumps of field grass.
Maybe God has a thrifty hand
takes hold of his meekest servants
shrinks them
til they are gone.

After the Church Service

we eat black and white cookies
bag apple strudel for my father.
He is not regular churchgoing
not since the Catholic orphanage days
when the stern forehead of denial first
tampered with his face.

I feel like the weight of sin has entered me.
My smart father's disappointed life
his dead mother, alcoholic dad
how some things never pass away
into a field of sweet grass.
The three family house, no car
too many jobs.
We hardly see him except on Sunday.

God forgives us our trespasses
my mother tells me
as if fallenness is a house with no stilts
a broken toy truck, the neglected doll
the world coming back to us
swollen with April
glued onto contrition's coat sleeves.

My mama shimmies into her pretty things
turns eggs, raises laundry onto the line
sullen-hipped
bending and unbending her day.
Is it pie-eyed to sit squat

beg the sun to enter
want to pin it up so high
that no one can displace it with
tire-gutted hands,
to believe just maybe angel food can
save me?

After school I disappear
down the basement
lock doors
sway my body back and forth
to the old crooner
pine like him
for *someone to watch over me.*

Some Sweaters

never grow warm wings.
My mother braided her life
into a parable of tea kettles, fried eggs
a waxy smile that denies the rain.

At midnight the girl with the
tulle and torn envelopes
parachutes onto roofs.
She has holes in her hands
is swarmed by birds
some filial deathbed
you have culled for her.

The earth gets tired of machines.
Grows cracks like a seam-sung woman.
It takes years for the skin
to grow back again.

Desperation has many faces.

Mary Jo

Mary Jo wore a colored bandana
over her hair
banana yellow
not to go with her shoes
but to set them off
like little fire engines
with flames on them.

Three weeks past her First Communion
God came for her with his torn wings.
I remember the date—May 15th.
Two months before my eighth birthday.
I remember the envelope of happiness
she always dug out of the yard's damp fist
as if there was no father chucking beer cans
no mother with yellowed teeth
tobacco-stained hands.

We played hide and seek
once the clothesline of days lengthened.
I could never find her.
She knew how to grow so small
she could erase herself behind tree limbs
inside boxes, shelf drawers
til one day she wouldn't be here anymore.

Is it a comfort to become invisible?
My father says *not everybody is meant to breathe*
the shrunken air here
live their days with even shoelaces

a scarcity of shade.
That sometimes it is the rarified space
that saves us
like metal crucifixes
plastic bags.
She chose a plastic bag.
Its clear circumference.
Tied one over her head
tried to find that perfect bubble
she could live in.
A membrane so impenetrable
you can outlast the rain.

You Find Your First Pair

crumbled leather
the toes pressed in where the cramped
feet claimed them
not yet heir to the terrible monotony
of grown-up days
still mud-inspired
puddle-proved
you tied the braided cord to the arm
of box tree
jumped rope through April's rain showers
as if the sky and the earth needed you

the pendulum slope of the rope line
sending you airborne after the
toe-tip clench of hard dirt
as if there was no nightfall
no dinner hour with its hasty provisions
no father who would walk away
from your life with his hands bleeding
no mother left lacing shoes
stitching on torn buttons
eating fudge-marble ice cream late night
when the solace of angels
was permanently driven from her ledge
and every day became
a screw-on jeans
kind of affair
efficient and terribly arresting
not handcuffed to God
but an invisible
kind of laundering

History Lesson

My father never married my mother.
People said that made me a bastard
and my mother a forlorn woman.
At night alone on the porch swing
she sang the sparrows to sleep.
Polished her red nails into picket fences.
For years my father's feet flitted
in and out the door
burdened with candy
the crumpled-down lip
of the roses.

They say that the earth grows
out of a green pelvis
and *lucky in love* is really an
abbreviation for solid thirst
the tenacity to make sure
all things breath in you.
But I say *lucky in love* is a footnote
to the world's geometry.
A rare bird.

My mother breathed lust
into her body's indentures
stuffed us in galoshes, yellow macs
tried to perish the rain.
Prayed for St. Jude to save us.
Our busted screen door
never got glued back
in her name.

The Priest at the Holy Redemption Church

says that the eye must be toothpicked open
clear as an unsotted river to find God.
His Sunday best is always enough for him.
I keep looking in the wrong places.
Upending cans, plastic play toys
the day's torn missiles of happiness
that wear abject feet
refuse to erase the inclemency of rain.

My sixth grade teacher says that
boldness has to do with getting your facts straight
careful analysis
that the history dates we memorize
are not just facts crammed down
our throats
but a way to make the world palpable
even-gaited
able to pitchfork the snow.

My day swings like this.
A pendulum of fabricated notions.
The history teacher with her implacable face.
The bottles of Coke we gurgle in the lunchroom
after the nutrition lecture.
The way I devour sin
because I am my father's child
and my parents only pretend to love each other
and the world might become wicked
if I throw crowbars in the wind
say what I think here.

When I grow up
I will play heretic
fabricate the color of angel wings
thistle
stumble past graves so preset
there will be nobody left
to shovel them back
into snow.

We Say *Hallelujah*

he wants us to
the minister who says
Christ needs the grand entry
certain throne to our hearts.

I mix cake flour, egg whites.
Whip angel food into the pillars
of heaven.
Will do anything to be perfect and guileless
in my father's kitchen.

Come August my mother gets hit
by a car.
My father takes out his shoe polish kit
buffs his loafers so shiny
my brother and I can see our faces in them.
I proposition the night to be
a peephole I can see through
make every stuffed creature into
an amicable rabbit with no fur bleeding.

My brother and I can go on forever
with our angel food cupcakes and solid words.
My father makes the church
into a house for us
grinds marble into glass eyes we can see by.
His sermons are rock hard.
You can trespass them with a child's hand
give your life over to them.

I dig hope out of my side pocket.
That sad damp soliloquy.
Proposition my nylon stockings to stop
making runs up and down my legs.
Become a gadfly. Street post. World weary.
The comet with an uncatchable tail.
We scribble our names for heaven.

Nobody can read them for the tarnished lines
that we thread.

My Birthday

is an exaggerated affair.
Everyone in my family trying to make up
for the absences that grieve me.

I blow out candles—14 of them—
imagine the world round and solvent as
unspoilt house trim.

July weeps the regrets of another heat wave.
The steering wheel hot in my mother's hands.
My father grabs another beer
erases his past, spells dissolution
into the web chair.

We prune our words
the way some people scalp roses
avoid the prickly spine of thistle
til the talk is of concrete things—
the weather, too much grizzle on the pork chops.
I learn to grow invisible
as a pale wind.

Later, my brother shoots white powder
into his veins.
I grow up and marry a lot.
Try to find God pinned on every clothesline.
Will learn that vanishing has its part to play
like incorrigible words erased from the
chalkboard's chaste skin
our distinct personalities no longer
invincible to shine.

There's a Gold Ladder

You climb up to God on it.
In heaven our appetites grow meek as kittens.
Nobody cares about the all-wheel drive truck
you coveted next door.
The priest told us that.
He held the wood cross snug to breaking.

That was years ago.
When I begged the confessional to save me.
Sang *Gloria* into the apartment's clenched breath
the July window fans working overtime to deliver
my mother from the life that she'd made here
our busted screen doors, her curvy body
in the low-cut Sunday dresses
singing another kind of hallelujah
out of the church pews.

Winters came and went.
The pink flamingos dug up
then pressed back in yard dirt.
My mother's tailgates of repentance towing.
At seventeen I find a boyfriend who can
show me another kind of heaven.
My brother finds powder
whiter than angel's wings.
My orphaned father loses his job
never finds another full-time one
confirms to himself nothing will save us.
A few years later I go on a college exchange
program to England

stay there for eight years
try to erase my past
the way some people erase their future.
My mother did that.
I long to believe in the God of missionary hands,
that my mother is circled by gulls
a benevolent sea-cleaving,
that nothing dies of disuse
gets turned away and
unbeknownst to me
my boat has already come in
with its billowed sails.

I wake up one morning
stunned with light
seduced by the garden's peonies
the wild lupin
less afraid of my past
the might of your quiet
inflammatory
hands.

My Brother Tells Me

he stays up half the night
prays for me
turns blue beads in his hand
wonders where my guts are
why I don't leave this house
walk away
surreptitious in my blue robes.

In winter there is nothing
my father won't do with the
pedestrian arrogance of his hands.
He makes a bonfire out of midnight.
Burns my dead mother's yellow dresses.
I pitch a tent against madness.
Am found sleepwalking
in my white muslin
with the sloped hem.

Every cadence a *loves me, loves me not*
kind of thing.
Each petal plucked clean
cut back naked to the stem.
I look in the mirror.
See my body pale as soap.
Listen to my brother's prayers for me.
The *Our Fathers, Hail Marys*.

Later there will be nothing
I can't do

with the raw terror of your hands.
The jet black midnight
God has
inscribed on me.

The Nickname *Little Dagger of Nothing* Impels Mary Beth to Staple Groves of Dining Needles onto the Wall

It started out harmlessly enough.
Age three raiding the pantry of its pound cake
the jam jars locked in lids
she wanted to free.
Father said it to her
while wiping the raspberry
off her hands—
you little dagger of nothing.

Afterwards the name sticks
follows her into the turtle sandbox
the shark-syringed water
follows her into the vanilla wafers
their collapsed creme tongues
til one day she's had enough—
takes off her tulle
her rhinestone barrettes
her pointy toe shoes with the red studs
grabs her paintbox
begins brushing dining needles
staples their shiny bodies over the walls.
The house swoons with them.
Transparent wings swamp the sideboard
cluster over the kitchen counter
cargo up the stairway that leads
to her mother and father's room
where the nests of eggs are hatching.
Thousands of them.

Within a week the house is
littered with painted insects.
Mary Beth feels free.
Almost buoyant.
Indestructible.
As if all manner of famine, catastrophe
have bypassed her body's exuberance.

Even after the walls are whitewashed
in eggshell
erased of the paintbox travesties
Mary Beth's parents cannot erase
the incendiary halo
that now hives a home in her head.

Part Four

*The Perilous Undertakings
of the Everyday World*

Aggregate of Stone

The bow weighted down
my suffragette morning slippers in
a lump by the door.
I dig reprisal out of the bed sheets.
Lathe you in soft rubbed thistle
the prerogative of a woman
to bathe and lounge
once the dismissal of the world
sets in.

By 10 a.m. our children climb in
huggle under the bed sheets.
Gather us on both sides
as if love is a morning cereal
their daily bread
and we—despite our mortal failings—
for better or worse
are heir to their kingdom
the homily
and the attrition.

Will even prayer count for enough
when the rain sets in?

Pregnant Again

I listen to you.
Banish my tongue.
Remember my dead mother
the soiled past, winter coming
single parenthood with the heat
turned low.

Remove her almost as fast as she
is placed here.
The young girl I will never know.
Sister of the boy who has come through
hailstorms.

Ten years pass.
I adopt a four-year-old girl child from China.
She is beautiful
gathers lost beads.
To my son she is *sister*.
In my heart she is *a resurrected boat*.

I build an altar in my heart's earlobe
a brick wall to keep you
forever apart from me
like those tiresome men who epigraph
a woman as *high maintenance*
and stridently walk away.

No one knows the courage God has given me.
I am saved, risen, divine

devoured, abject
sometimes perishable.

No man matches
the soft ardor
of your torso's burning.

The Perilous Undertakings
of the Everyday World

This morning the cat scratched
my seven-year-old daughter across
her chest and neckline.
She who loves him more than the world,
runs her fingers daily up and down
the fur of his sleek chin.

We had heard it before
love with its useful tongue
flapping
almost palpable
almost candles at midnight
the belief that industry
sits on swing doors
and every dance floor needs us
with our perilous shoes burning.

It is almost August.
The heat drags its thirsty tongue
over the tarmac.
All day our dog keeps his distance
from the cat's arching.
My daughter approaches with hesitant words
as if betrayal has a double wingspan
and love won't always save us
keep us durable against the rain.

When the World Wears
Its Gyro Fantasmical Glasses

and pierces the moon for its bed
we hear *we shall overcome*
over the airwaves.
Resolute as certain soldiers
asked to vanquish what's thrust at them.
I don't know my way around happiness anymore.
Like a lost language it slips
into the soil of my bed sheets
the day's sore feet.
My brother says *nothing escapes*
the redeemed eye
and every hour is a field of hyacinth
for those who pray here.

I am the unconverted one
the sinner who spawns collapsed wheels
hastily tied shoestrings
moves in and out of the foster home
the woman with a cardboard house
nailed to her shoes
believe it takes more than sermons
to bring heaven into our door.

June wields rain as infested as hard balls
the boys at the Immaculate Conception School
used to aim straight for our heads.
There is a fierce love some girls
find here.

I rototil the garden.
Turn in winter's cover crop.
Imagine mescalin greens grown as
ungainly and wild as heaven.
The two garden plots my children will tend here.
Our bok choy, squash, cucumber vines
spreading clear out into the blackberries.

Can an encyclopedic eye
speak to us?
Can we pepper the world with other kinds
of remembrance
some torn deliverance of hope
that street children cling to?
You scoff at my dilapidated
version of paradise
as if a cross bleeds on my palms
and nothing rank or dissolved
will speak for us.

It is June.
I want to believe whatever crawls
can walk again
that what we give
will come back to us
from an unfisted grave.
That God likes nothing better
than bok choy and collapsible boys
girls with poppies in their hands
a vague knowledge
some shiny pinned allegiance
to what's been placed here.

Pink—Such a Frittery Color

My daughter's ambition for a scarf
that is fu fu
rides down to her backside.

She dreams of eight candles
chocolate on chocolate
the scarf she knows I am knitting her.
Imagines it will be braided
silky as ropelines
attached to ancient Chinese bridges.

Her black hair grown long
shiny down to her waist.
When I watch her move I am sure that God
is in love with dancers
and it is back inside our bodies
that other paradise
will be found.

She is counting the days.
Not as a contingent for happiness
but simply an addendum
to that song.

No Use Cursing the Day

It is July.
Hummingbirds land on my feeder.
I remember my mother
her shaved dresshems
penchant for children,
pin butcher-block paper to the walls
take out my ladybug paint set.
The black ink that must substitute
for heaven.
Pitch black. Only the stars bleeding.

Antelopes, foxy wolves, snow bears
sleighs traveling over tundra walls.
The mittened child in the corner of the hill
barely perceptible with her snow globe
and icy breath
the way each drift
lost star claims her.

It turns out not every animal body
every seal skin in this world
is destined
to vanish away.

Staggered across
these sanguine walls
they shine.

I Will Call You a Criminal
for Ransacking My Bed

She told him that. Cheeky.
Packed her bags.
He obsessed over the ingratitude.
She fled out the door.

How many *Our Fathers, Hail Marys* will
make the tabernacle genuflect in our hands?
Can a leaking radiator converse to us
about the disposition of the moon?
Will the girl with caspian notions of happiness
moan the field mouse at her door,
clip lupin gathering their thinly disguised
purples into the night's sweet shade?

Her mother told her *it takes handling a shitload of pain*
to live here. She knew that.
Her mother cramped for years in the three family house
spooning nothing out of the shelf jars.
The angry schism of her father's hot breath.

Maybe God loves this one—who tied a noose
around her neck
decided not to die here
the one who knows that lastness
is not the cripple's epitaph
but the throne of ivy, lush as perpetual summer
the creeping worrisome weed, foreign invader some
people disdain
weaving its delicate lurid fingers endlessly
across the earth's green plate.

Can You Imagine God

clamping his hands on your throat
cleaving to the bitter root of a past
that refuses to come clean.

I burn bacon so crisp it
erases the fat in its skin
crumble it in the German potato salad
my father once made with his
summer hands.

As a child I learned to collect pebbles
broken shells
wedge them in my throat
like a stop-gap
til I was a mute bird fasting.
They say fasting is more than
the road to denial
that emptiness is a favor returned
a homage to God's love for us.

It is July.
I cook bacon.
Crumble it for the potato salad I won't eat
that my children yearn for.
They are eight and eleven.
Know that anguish can have tread feet
become a stick figure
bony as God's love for us.
That some things are hard to come right
in this world.

Know there are wilted squash vines
slug-devoured pole beans
treacheries even the cool cotton
of our beds can't change.
We stumble into daylight.
Place pebbles around the clay sculptures of women
handfuls of dinked sand dollars, poems
spread them over the yard paths
our good luck chimeras
reminding us
it is a gift to be here
not straight-hung
as perfect souls with no pitch in them
but salient
a string of chipped beach shells
combing the wind's deft face.

Part Five

The Body's Lasting Allegiance to Snow

Somewhere off Jennings Avenue

there is a girl wearing
shoes dyed the color of lemons
lavender dress hems.
She is not afraid of their aimless flirtation
the exuberant way the butterflies
float their wings over the flower's loose hair.

It is a skunk cabbage kind of day
fiddling with her terrible fancies
almost disdaining the width of things.
No ho-hum profusion of rain.
No plastic purple octopus collapsed in a puddle
by the forsythia's wet tongue.

She tells the sun—*I will lure you*
on red licorice
mincemeat pie
from my mother's kitchen.
I will build a snug house
with giant windows
so the sky
can find me.
My door wide open.
Then I will be vacant.
Vacant but lasting.

It is April.
The ground grown muddy from taking in
more water than it can hold.
The Willamette River murky

a bulge of swelled tree limbs
torn from their roots.
The petals of tulip, camellia
holding on
with their shrunken breath.
In the galaxy of light
she builds a house with nine windows.
Hangs up polkadot curtains.
Lets her dolls play there
their long black hair shiny as seal skin
matted as the dog's cuff on them.
She tells her wisest frog—
when I grow up I will
shrink as perfect as small boxes
lined in delicate tissue breath
tiny as crickets who rub their legs
in the wind
worship the sound of the smallest
flea dancing.

She grew up.
Grew large then small again.
Lives in a house with 9 windows
2 dogs, 1 cat, 3 gold fish
and many children
a lapidary of dolls weaving.
The sun seldom refuses
to enter her room.
The polkadot curtains have faded
but not her shoes
not the butterflies floating their wings
above the flower's loose hair.

Already the Garden's Ranunculus
Have Cast a Weary Face
Toward April's Loose Skin

You can indict a past
squeeze grey out of the worn down
coat sleeves
forget the doll cake tiered in
three layers of pink icing
the muck of machinery
the nuns retinue of prayers
to bring God's blessing back
from the accursed home
forge lust out of the
sunken anvils
the orphaned father
the mother who keeps reinventing
rooms trying to find her
original face in them.

My children's eighth and tenth birthdays
remind me of another year slipped away
the ranunculus' dying annotations.
I rub my hands as if
friction can light fire
mend marriages
ignite the past into something
more durable I can live by.
You remind me of my nuptial with death
the way God clambers up every stairway
finds the yellow envelope
enters my heart.

When I Was Called Up Yesterday

not for my gallantry
but for my cursed breath
told to get my *house in order*
my act straight
it was not out of piquance
I confronted you
but more from a lost tail
a sense it takes a stalwart kind of
allegiance to be here
minding the city's loose teeth
the fact that so many come to
so little in this world.

If God is a stopwatch that
seizes the brain
reorders the left and the right chemistry
the schism between loneliness
and approbation
then I am wearing tennis shoes
trying to unfasten the rain
count on more than good luck sermons
anoint my dead mother's blue eyes on me.

In April the Northwest is mud grey.
Everything seems derelict
as the wind.
I proposition death to wear soft shoes
tiptoe around the house's demise
my steadfast version of happiness
that has cleats in it

rancorous angels that stumble past midnight
and razor the stars' repose.

I spell you out of my hands'
faulty allegiances
as if what we find here is what we get.

All my clotheslines emptied and billowing.

I am the barefoot girl
trellised to snowfall, fledgling roses
the stampede of blossoms
the yellow watering can
wedded to my hands.

Maybe I Have Been Seeking God
in All the Wrong Places

A sparrow with its wings
chopped off.
The house assails me.
Parsimonious light.
The vagrance of winter.
His hands that excavate holes
bury the roots of trees
always depart
an exit door swinging
on a perpetual hinge.

There is an indenture so dark
the night can't consume it
it preys on tenuous voices
soft sleeves
the alliteration of nothing
in a blowfish world.

I cup my ears around emptiness
feel the weight of it
like something laid carefully
in a dresser wrapped in lace.
Disdain the day's closed shoes.

My body turns south.
I practice penitence.
Paint my nails thin.
Every rock becomes

a sun pierced ledge
I can see the world by
indecent as the love
you've banked for me.

I Call Midnight

out of my side pockets.
Press Virgin Mary icons onto the wall.
Refuse to sit in a fish bowl
with my lust bleeding
let somebody else's sense of something
speak for me—
meadowlark of plenty in a bulging world.

I strip sheets.
Hoe squash beds.
Remember the this and that
I came for.
The disgruntled shoe.
The circumstance of plenty
that passes for heaven.
Know that the deft ear
is not a prelude to this one.

The day longs to right itself
feline on purring knees.
My past comes back to me
some unassailable equator
surreptitious in red shoes.

I Will Pray for You, He Said

as if I was a lusty cousin of dilapidation
a porridgeless child
the product of sin in a rock solid world.

I learn to drown in the moon's loose skin
step carefully around the heads of the roses.
Make a nest of feathered duff in the cracks
between loneliness. Cast a line for
the sky's sweet tongue. Grow alfalfa.
Make salad sandwiches.
Let the past knead me with its castoff wings.

Now each day is a candlelight
kind of affair.
The night's torrential rain pawing.
The flakes of snow in my glass ball
a storm of white fluttering.
As if nothing can be something in the right hands
and there are quiet epiphanies
that can becalm the palm reader's
crystal ball
the calico of happiness
as God stumbles stubbornly
in and out of my door.

They Prayed for Me

like they would any sinner.
I was buttressed, reformed
made more than perfunctory
sworn to be born again
in your breath.

My tailgates stop bleeding.
The rufus redtail sets up a home in our tree.
I call on strangers. Brew tea. Dust off the bamboo tray.
Collapse the dead peonies somebody else
bequeathed for me.

Now I float above water
stand guard over the garden's profuse beds.
The lettuce, basil, bok choy
bolt their way toward heaven
on sun-soaked wings.
Fledgling squash vines escape
the slug's slick tongue.
Black spot weakens
on the petals of the roses.

Every song I've ever heard
no longer a tirade against disaster
but piquant
littered with new radish leaves
the dog's welcoming tail.

When You Pass by the Gatepost

to easy happiness
the birds first look in disdain
at the tawdry color of your wings
the ground shakes down wormed apples
dead fall
and every promise
is a hairpin turn between
loss and finding heaven.

Nobody told you about
discontent
grey clouds littering their face
across the puddle's exuberance
the nailed-down windows
the prerogative of privilege
to slaughter what it lends.

You bypass your fate
step your foot into
the yard's raised beds
into hailstorms of another kind of happiness.
This day a sort of cryptic
mistletoe somebody
bent over your door
kissable even
amidst the absences
durable
as the crocus mating.

I Wanted God

to walk all over my body
seed me in paw prints
a colony of rose bushes

as if I could be made new again
like the prophets speak of
my this's and that's no longer towing
my desire to tap terrestrial out
of the darkest sheets.

One day I woke up mysterious.

Woke up invisible
sculpting women
writing poems the world wants to forget.

God tore a rasp from my hair.
It was no longer fashionable to live
in the world's coat sleeves.

I gave up digging yard holes
trying to inflate rubber ducks in square ponds.

It is surprising what the seasons can do to me.

I tell the sky—
I will be the girl
who keeps every host under her tongue
till I am a bird with faithful wings
a speck of magenta on a
serge blue dress kind of day.

Ambrosia

Midnight without any blinds on it.

The delirious moment when
your fingers fan more than enamel
capture me by surprise in the soft nook
of your sloped waistband.

The pared-down chime of it.
God riding ambrosia over every good thing

til I am fearless
an animal devoid of rancor

not needle flinging
only this pawing
easy injunction

to nuzzle and lick.

For Those of Us Who Persist to Contemplate Magic in a Damped-Down World

You tell me about the loose tongue
that lets you snow-shovel heaven
as if there is no tomorrow
no world breaking
and the black night holds
every vestige of the moon's
sweet cakes like sorghum in
a consummated field.

In October nothing anguishes you
not the leaf fall
the letterpress of happiness that
stamps lust on our palms
not the pumpkins wheelbarrowed
and carted away
their faces that will be carved up
propped out on porch stoops
displayed as an emblem
of how desecration can shine.

After Her Reprieve Saves Her

You punctuate the moon
have your own elliptical stars
as if the world needs coaxing
an unsteady hand
the outrageous tongue's machinery
and whoever slit her wrist so many
years ago—
it won't happen again—
she turned into bird pecks
mule dust
terrestrial feet
an avuncular heave of the eye's
starlight.

Vandal of coat factories
emissary of jocular children.
Now you never take *no* for an answer
know that paintboxes are for more
than just plastering
that every day rinses salt from your eyes
lets you witness heaven
from a jagged ledge.

Offering

All manner of good wishes
that's what she wanted for him.
The unbridled tongue
time with its snipped-off edges
and the semester of young girls
beckoning.
Surely the seasons
hadn't evaded her completely
with their slate steps—
the garden's unangular repose.

I will worship the moon
she told herself
and eyelet cotton and
God with his hands bent
in the earth's derision
wielding compost for the roots' conferencing.

The evening primrose lumber their way
on sloped trellises toward heaven.
But it was not heaven
she would offer him
nor houses with their paintwork
pressed perfect as slotted machinery
or women without hysteria on their breath
the amber side of quiet's solitude.

Perhaps what she could offer him
from the dismounted day

was her chastened tongue
the world her hands created
out of clay and blue ink
her body's lasting allegiance to snow.

One Day I Will Grow Up

with no name stamped to my head
no hasty deliberations.
I will walk into the past
and find ancient shoes
children sledding over the January mounds
of snow.

I wipe my eyes.
Am afraid to move there.

Will you come with me, I ask.

But I know it is a useless question.
That I will be buttressed by nothing
when I enter this sled.

The snow falling.
All my love of God held tight as
the metal gliders
attached to the frame.

About the Author

Toni Thomas' poems have been published in literary magazines in Austria, New Zealand, Canada, England, Scotland, and Australia. In the United States, her work has appeared in over fifty literary magazines, including *Prairie Schooner*, *North Dakota Quarterly*, *Hayden's Ferry Review*, *the minnesota review*, *Weber - The Contemporary West*, *Rhino*, *Notre Dame Review*, and *Poetry East*. She has received *Atlanta Review*'s International Merit Award and an Ann Stanford Poetry Prize from the *Southern California Review*. Her poems have twice been nominated by literary magazines for a Pushcart Prize. Her first chapbook, *Walking on Water*, was published by Finishing Line Press. Her second chapbook, *Fast as Lightning*, won the 2010 Gribble Press Poetry Competition. *Chosen* was a finalist in the 2010 Brick Road Poetry Press competition. Recently two additional full length manuscripts were finalists for the Anhinga Poetry Prize, the May Swenson Poetry Award, and the Crab Orchard Poetry Prize.

She lives in Oregon with her children and likes to contemplate the moon from her bed.

Our Mission

The mission of Brick Road Poetry Press is to publish and promote poetry that entertains, amuses, edifies and surprises a wide audience of appreciative readers. We are not qualified to judge who deserves to be published, so we concentrate on publishing what we enjoy. Our preference is for poetry geared toward dramatizing the human experience in language rich with sensory image and metaphor, recognizing that poetry can be, at one and the same time, both as familiar as the perspiration of daily labor and as outrageous as a carnival sideshow.

BRICK ROAD
POETRY PRESS

Also Available from Brick Road Poetry Press

www.brickroadpoetrypress.com

Dancing on the Rim by Clela Reed

Possible Crocodiles by Barry Marks

Pain Diary by Joseph D. Reich

Otherness by M. Ayodele Heath

Drunken Robins by David Oates

Damnatio Memoriae by Michael Meyerhofer

Lotus Buffet by Rupert Fike

The Melancholy MBA by Richard Donnelly

Etch and Blur by Jamie Thomas

About the Prize

The Brick Road Poetry Prize, established in 2010, is awarded annually for the best book-length poetry manuscript. Entries are accepted August 1st through November 1st. The winner receives $1000 and publication. For details on our preferences and the complete submission guidelines, please visit our website at www.brickroadpoetrypress.com.

www.ingramcontent.com/pod-product-compliance
Lightning Source LLC
Chambersburg PA
CBHW031857090426
42741CB00005B/538